©2016 Words of Wisdom Educational Consulting, 803 Hadley Ave
Old Hickory, TN
All rights reserved. No portion of this book may be reprinted or distributed without the express written permission of the authors. All photographs are the work of the authors unless otherwise indicated.

Hello Washington DC!

Keith Pruitt

*To Felicia
Thanks For Being
600!
Keith Pruitt
2017*

Words of Wisdom
2016

Table of Contents

Introduction	**Page 6**
Statues	**Page 7**
Buildings	**Page 9**
Monuments	**Page 20**
Museums	**Page 23**
Other Sites	**Page 25**
Conclusion	**Page 26**
Glossary	**Page 27**
Websites	**Page 29**

Introduction

The United States is a large country. The territory of the United States covers the forty-eight **contiguous** states, the state of Alaska that is west of Canada, the state of Hawaii that is in the Pacific Ocean, and various territories such as Puerto Rico and Guam. The **capital** of a country is where the government is headquartered. The seat of government of the United States is Washington, D.C. The D.C. stands for *District of Columbia*. This area of land was carved from Maryland and Virginia to become a special area to house the government that was not a part of any state.

Washington, D.C. is an exciting place to visit. There are so many special things to see there that one can only experience in the capital. Congress, both the House of Representatives and the Senate, meet in the **Capitol** to enact laws and oversee the creation of a budget. The Supreme Court, the highest court in the land, also meets in this city to review rulings of lower courts and to ascertain that these rulings have not violated the Constitution.

The President of the United States and the Vice-President also work and live in Washington. The President resides in The White House. The Vice President's residence was once the Naval Observatory. It is in the Embassy Row section of the city. The Vice President presides over the Senate. The President is the chief Executive of the country. He is the constitutional head of Executive Branch of government responsible for carrying out the laws enacted by Congress.

Much of what one sees in Washington, D.C. is a reminder of our history. Tributes of respect are given to former Presidents, generals, and soldiers who fought in various wars. The city also celebrates the importance of the arts in American culture.

My daughter and I love traveling to Washington, D.C. and wanted to share our nation with you in this book. We hope you enjoy reading about the various places we have been. We also hope you will learn a great deal about our country. And if you haven't been, we hope you too will get to enjoy our nation's capital.

Keith Pruitt

Statues

The **Treasury** Department is next to the White House and was one of the first four **cabinet** positions created under the Presidency of George Washington. Alexander Hamilton, whose **statue** is in the south courtyard of the Treasury building, was the first Secretary of the Treasury and perhaps the most important cabinet officer in shaping the Federalist **policies** that would govern the country for the first quarter century.

There are numerous statues around Washington, DC honoring Presidents, military leaders, and important persons in the history of the nation. One will find here statues honoring James Garfield, Marquis de Lafayette, and Dr. Martin Luther King, Jr. In fact, there are more than 110 statues in the District of Columbia and that doesn't count Statuary Hall in the Capitol Building.

The statues in Washington, DC honor political leaders, artists, military heroes of many wars, Presidents, religious leaders, **activists**, and many others whose contributions to America have been exemplar and lasting. There are even statues of people from many centuries ago whose influence in Europe and Asia left an indelible mark on society in the United States. Explore these on the internet and tell a friend about what you have learned regarding these statues.

This statue of Franklin Delano Roosevelt shows the great World War II leader sitting with his **cape** in a scene in the third term room of the Roosevelt Memorial. The President who served more years in office than any other President had been **stricken** with polio and could not walk. Also depicted in the scene is the Presidential dog, Fala. This memorial to President Roosevelt opened in 1997.

Numerous Presidents are honored by statues in the capital city. Do you know which statue of a President is the closest one to the White House?

Located across from the north side of the White House in the center of Lafayette Park, the **equestrian** Andrew Jackson statue honors his victory as a General at the Battle of New Orleans during the War of 1812. There are three of these statues of Jackson in existence. Do you know the location of the other two?

The other two are located in Jackson Square in New Orleans and the state capitol grounds in Nashville, Tennessee where Jackson served as a local hero as well as politician.

Buildings

Perhaps the most famous building in Washington, DC is the white structure at 1600 Pennsylvania Avenue known as The White House. At various periods it was known as The Executive Mansion. The John Adams family was the first to live in the Executive Mansion. The house looked very different then. The north and south **porticoes** had not been constructed—nor had the east and west wings.

The West Wing was constructed by order of Theodore Roosevelt in 1902. Until that time the President's office was located on the second floor mixed in with the living quarters. The East Wing as it appears today was built in 1942 by Franklin Roosevelt initially to cover the **bunker** built for protection of the President but also as an entrance for visitors to the White House.

The Truman balcony was added to the South Portico in the extensive renovations of the White House in 1948. It allows the First Family some ability to sit outside and enjoy the marvelous view of the Washington Monument which is directly across the park grounds from this balcony. Did you know that the entire White House was gutted during that renovation?

While to some visitors the White House seems smaller than imagined, the house contains a great deal of space with five floors and two mezzanines. The state rooms are the only parts of the home the public generally sees on a visit to the White House. This includes the State Dining Room, the East Room, the Chief Usher's Office (the overseer of the Executive Mansion), the Red Room, the Blue Room, and the Green Room. The main entrance here is into the Cross Hallway where the Grand Staircase is located. The entrance is the 1600 Pennsylvania Avenue Entrance on the north side. The Blue room opens to the South Portico.

There is a ground level entrance on the South Portico. This is the diplomatic reception entrance. On this floor is the Library, the China Room, and assorted office and storage areas. The second and third floors are the private **residence**. Most of these rooms are available for the first family to decorate as they wish. On the second floor are The Lincoln bedroom and the Queen's bedroom. These are considered historic rooms and are left in their historic form. These rooms may be accessed by a separate stairway and the section of rooms may be isolated by pocket doors to provide privacy for visiting guests.

Courtesy White House

Over 100 residence workers call The White House their place of **employment** from florist, chefs, housekeepers, dishwashers, butlers, valets, assistants, groundskeepers, carpenters and electricians. Many work in the White House for decades serving multiple numbers of First Families.

In the West Wing of the White House are the President's Oval Office and many of his staff members, members of the Press Corp and personal assistants such as the Chief of Staff. The East Wing houses the First Lady's staff as well as security measures for the President below ground.

Wherever the President and First Lady go in the White House, they are surrounded by security and people attending to their every need. If you are an adult child of the President's paying a visit, you will pay for your own meals!

Next to the White House is a large strange gray building known as the Eisenhower Executive Office Building. Built between 1871-1888, the office building was constructed to house the State, War, and Navy departments of government. Today the building houses many of the White House office staff. During the Nixon **administration**, the President maintained a working office in this building reserving the Oval Office for **ceremonial** occasions.

On the Arlington, Virginia side of the Potomac River lies one of the great structures of government—the Pentagon. The building houses the operational departments of the United States military. The structure is next to Arlington National Cemetery and the section facing the cemetery was attacked in the September 11, 2001 terrorist attacks. How many sides are there to this building? Who do you think you would find in this building? Would they be wearing any kind of uniform? Do you know what the different branches of service are called?

Construction on the United States Capitol building began in 1793 when it was decided to remove the capital from New York City to a newly created District of Columbia in a city named in honor of President George Washington. The building has grown through the years. The dome was incomplete when Lincoln was first inaugurated on its steps in 1861. The wings have been added over time. The Supreme Court also met in this building originally until a separate building was constructed in 1935.

The National Cathedral to the northwest of the White House is an **enormous** church building of historical importance. It is the final resting place of the only President to be buried in Washington DC and the scene of many historic events including the state funeral of President Ronald Reagan. It took 83 years to build the cathedral. Its central tower stands 30 stories tall and the structure has 231 stained glass windows. Do you know which President is entombed here? Can you guess how many gargoyles there are in the structure? How about angels?

If you said President Woodrow Wilson is entombed at the National Cathedral, you are correct. President Wilson served during World War I. He died in 1924. But he is not the only **notable** to be buried here. Helen Keller, Anne Sullivan, former Secretary of State Cordell Hull and Senator Stewart Symington are all buried at the Cathedral.

The Supreme Court building (next page) stands just north of the Capitol building and is beside the National Library of Congress. The building was erected in 1935 as the permanent house of the nation's highest court. It was in this building that Gore v Bush was decided ending the dispute over the 2000 election. Do you know how many justices currently serve on the Supreme Court? Since 1960, there have been but four Chief Justices of the Supreme Court: Earl Warren, Warren Burger, William Rehnquist, and the current John Roberts.

The Supreme Court is the nation's highest court making decisions as to the constitutionality of laws passed by states and Congress and ruling in criminal matters as the final right of **appeal**. It takes a mere five votes on the court to render a decision.

The building below is Ford's Theater famous for something very horrible which happened there. It was in this building on Good Friday, April 19, 1865 while attending the play *Our American Cousin* that Abraham Lincoln was assassinated. He died the next morning across the street in the Petersen Boarding House. Both of these are open to the public and contain exciting museums where you will be able to see the very gun that Booth used in the shooting. The picture to the right is a recreation of the VIP booth where Lincoln was shot.

The second picture on the previous page was taken from the doorway leading from the dress circle into the VIP sitting area where President and Mrs. Lincoln were sitting. This would have been approximately the same position taken up by John Wilkes Booth just seconds before he shot the President. Above is the gun he used and to the right is the President's viewing box from the Dress Circle.

The only other President to be shot in Washington, DC was President James Garfield who was shot in the back at the old train station which has since been torn down.

There are two buildings standing along the Potomac River as one goes toward Georgetown that hold great significance. The buildings are side by side: The Kennedy Center and The Watergate.

The Kennedy Center was built as a theater for the arts and opened in 1971. It is named in honor of President John F Kennedy. Each year around Christmas, the center holds a star-studded **gala** honoring legendary entertainers of stage, screen and theater. These galas are always attended by the President and First Lady who sit with the honorees.

In its performance theaters one would find performances by the National Symphony, a ballet company, and numerous concerts. The Kennedy Center has honored the careers of some 185 entertainers from Roy Acuff to Ella Fitzgerald since the inception of the Kennedy Center Honors in 1978.

This strange looking building is The Watergate Hotel and Office Complex. It was here in 1972 that burglars connected to the re-election campaign of President Richard Nixon were caught breaking into Democratic National Headquarters. The cover-up of White House involvement eventually led to President Nixon's **resignation** on August 9, 1974.

Today the building still serves as offices for many companies and also houses a hotel. The building sits on the banks of the Potomac River near the Kennedy Center and the Lincoln Memorial.

There are many historic homes in the DC area. Among them are the Wilson House on S Street, the Octagon (where President Madison signed the **treaty** ending the War of 1812), numerous embassies, and this Greek Revival house in Arlington across the Potomac from the Lincoln Memorial. The house was once home to General Robert E. Lee one of the greatest generals in American history. At the start of the Civil War, Lee decided he would fight for whichever side Virginia sided with which happened to be the Confederacy. President Lincoln ordered the land and house to be seized and it was turned into a burial ground for soldiers killed in the battle. It became Arlington National Cemetery. Many notables of American history are buried here including President and Chief Justice William Howard Taft and President John F. Kennedy.

All those buried at Arlington have some connection with the military service or political service to the American people. Among other notables buried there are Joe Louis, Nixon Attorney General John Mitchell,

and Supreme Court Justice Oliver Wendell Holmes as well as many other military heroes such as Audie Murphey, General John Pershing, General Omar Bradley, Senator Ted Kennedy, Senator Robert Kennedy, Admiral Hyman Rickover, Chief Justice Warren Burger, Chief Justice William Rehnquist, General David Jones, Robert Lincoln (son of President Lincoln), Justice Thurgood Marshall, and Justice William O Douglas. There are more than 400,000 graves in the 600 plus acres. Who are these people?

One of the most visited sites in Arlington National Cemetery is a place where the name of the dead is unknown. It is called the Tomb of the Unknowns. A guard has stood over the grave of these soldiers since 1937. These unknown soldiers are from World Wars I and II and the Korean War.

Also located in Arlington National Cemetery are monuments paying tribute to those lost in national disasters. There is a monument to the *USS Maine*, the Space Shuttle Columbia, and the Space Shuttle Challenger.

Located in a newer portion of the cemetery is a monument to those lost at the Pentagon on September 11, 2001.

When you go to Arlington National Cemetery you will want to have plenty of time because there are many things to see there including the changing of the guard. There are shuttles that will take you around the grounds but there will still be a great deal of walking. There is also a museum both in the welcome center and in the theatre to help explain the things you will see.

Monuments

A monument is something built to honor a person. Washington DC is often referred to as the *city of monuments*. There are several monuments in the city that have become the largest attractions for visitors. These monuments are **illuminated** at night their white marble seemingly glowing for those entering the city.

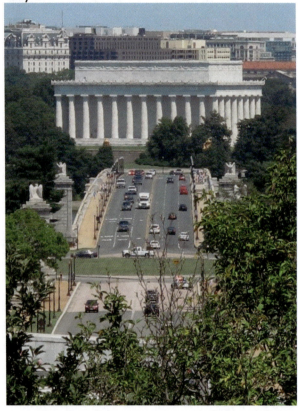

One of the most beloved of the memorials is that built at the end of the Memorial Bridge coming from Arlington National Cemetery. The Lincoln Memorial is a Greek Revivalist structure near the banks of the Potomac River. The tribute to the 16th President Abraham Lincoln was conceived in the late 1860s not long after Lincoln's assassination but the building did not begin construction until 1914. The monument was completed in 1922.

On the north side of the large structure are steps leading from the reflecting pool up to the inside of the monument. There are 87 steps. It was at the top of these steps that Martin Luther King, Jr. delivered his *I Have A Dream Speech*. When one goes into the inside of the monument, there is a large statue of Abraham Lincoln sitting in a large chair. Around the inside of the monument are a number of Lincoln's famous *sound bites.*

These noted sayings are from Lincoln's most famous speeches. The design of this monument was intended to be in line at one end of the national mall with the Washington Monument and then the Capitol building at the other end of the mall all lining up. The Washington Monument towers 555 feet into the Washington sky and was completed in 1884. Construction began in 1848 during the Presidency of James K Polk. Through the years the construction was interrupted by the Civil War and political strife. When it was completed, the Washington Monument honoring America's first President was the tallest building in the world.

Between the Lincoln Memorial and the area of the Washington obelisk are the Vietnam Wall, the World War II Memorial, Korean War Veterans Memorial, and the Martin Luther King, Jr. Memorial located by the Tidal Basin. There are also some smaller memorials to notable individuals such as Albert Einstein and John Ericcson.

Were one to stand on the Truman Balcony of the White House looking directly south toward the Potomac River, one would be overwhelmed by the tremendous height of the Washington Monument. There are windows at the very top of the monument which are accessed by an elevator ride to the top. At night at the top of the monument, if one looks toward the Arlington Cemetery, the eternal flame on the grave of President John F. Kennedy is visible.

Directly south of the Washington Monument at the edge of the Tidal Basin is located a monument to our nation's third President and the author of the Declaration of Independence—Thomas Jefferson. Construction of the Monument which mirrors the architectural style made famous by Jefferson's Monticello and the Rotunda at the University of Virginia, was begun in 1939 and completed four years later. The statue of Jefferson that graces the center of the structure was added in 1947.

There are other monuments that dot the landscape of DC. There are monuments honoring the Boy Scouts, Samuel Gompers, President Franklin Roosevelt, George Mason, Robert Taft, Chief Justice John Marshall, and multitudes of other **prominent** people and honoring specific events.

At the current time plans are underway to erect a Ronald Reagan Memorial in Washington DC. Over time there will surely be other memorials and statues added to the landscape. Currently if one were to spend just half an hour at each monument in Washington DC, it would take over 50 hours just to see them all.

Museums

Washington DC is filled with all types of museums. From the grand museums of the Smithsonian to the art museums, there is much to see in this city. One of the most popular museums for kids is the National Space and Aeronautics Museum on the mall. Housing some of the **artifacts** of America's history of flight, this museum is a crowd pleaser. One may also check out the Museum of Natural History, the Museum of American History, the American Indian Museum, the Holocaust Museum, the National Archive, the Library of Congress, the American Art Museum, the African American History and Culture Museum, the Hirschhorn Museum and Sculpture Garden, the Portrait Gallery, The Castle, and others that are along the mall.

One can also tour the Capital Building and see Statutory Hall. Tours of the White House are somewhat limited for security reasons but these do still happen. There is also the National Gallery of Art, the Daughters of the American Revolution Museum, the International Spy Museum, Madame Tussauds Wax Museum, Woodrow Wilson's House on S Street, the Newseum, and the Octagon House. This is by no means an exclusive list of museums or historic houses to visit. The National Zoo, operated by the Smithsonian is not far away from DC and there is also another air and space museum located near Dulles Airport.

Newseum on the left and statue from Museum of American Indians

This is one of the many **ornate** rooms in the Custis-Lee mansion in Arlington. The Arlington House had belonged to General Robert E. Lee before the Civil War but was **confiscated** by the United States Government as punishment for his serving in the Union Army. The location is now Arlington National Cemetery and The Robert E. Lee Memorial. The House was originally built by George Washington Parke Custis, the biological grandson of Martha Custis Washington. He was adopted by George Washington as a son. Custis' daughter Mary Anna was married to Robert E. Lee.

Other Sites

The Old Congressional Cemetery is also an interesting place to visit. Here one will find the final resting place of FBI Director J. Edgar Hoover and John Philip Sousa.

Statue of Martin Luther in front of church located in Thomas Square

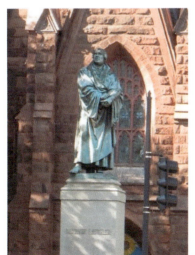

The West Wing of the White House

Conclusion

Washington, DC is filled with so many wonderful sights to see and great adventures to take in. There are organized tours that will transport one from place to place or one can take foot tours to many locations. If sports excite you, one can take in basketball, football, baseball, hockey, and women's basketball on the professional level as well as nationally known college sports from Georgetown or the University of Maryland. DC also has plenty of venues for eating and entertainment.

Cherry Blossom time is a favored time for capital travel as over 3,000 trees blossom all over the city bringing an unparalleled brilliance. Summers can be uncomfortable because of the heat and humidity, but it is a great time to experience the city as well. Because there is so much walking, one will find cart vendors set up along the mall grounds where you can stay hydrated.

There is so much to do in this city. Even multiple trips there will find you still finding more and more to do. There may be some obstacles such as traffic and parking but a family vacation to the nation's capital should be on everyone's short list of *must take* trips.

We hope you have enjoyed our adventure to Washington, DC and that it has created in you a desire to experience the city yourself. This isn't an exhaustive book of even our adventures there, and we have many more adventures yet to experience. We wish you happy learning and happy travels.

Glossary

Activists-A person who tries to change things in society that they believe aren't right.

Administration-Those entrusted with the control of executive or governing powers.

Appeal-Requesting a higher court to reverse a decision.

Artifacts-An object of cultural or historical interest.

Bunker-A defensive fortification built for the protection of people. They are usually constructed below ground.

Cabinet-A group of advisers to the President of the United States.

Cape-An article of clothing generally thrown over the shoulders without sleeves.

Capital-The city in which the seat of government resides.

Capitol-A building housing the legislature.

Ceremonial-A formal ritual.

Confiscated-To take something from another by the authority of government.

Contiguous-Sharing a common border, touching one another.

Employment-A Job, a person's occupation.

Enormous-Large, vast in size.

Equestrian-Having to do with riding a horse.

Gala-A celebration or party with entertainment.

Illuminated-To light up.

Notable-One who is worthy of notice, a famous person.

Ornate-Intricate, elaborate, fancy.

Policies-A statement of belief or action that is intended.

Porticoes-A porch attached to a building with columns.

Prominent-An important person, well known.

Residence-Where a person lives, the building in which one lives.

Resignation-The act of giving up a position, to quit.

Statue-A representation of a person made from a metal, wood, or stone.

Stricken-to be affected or afflicted by a bad condition.

Treasury-The collective funds of a government or organization.

Treaty-An agreement between two parties or nations.

Websites

The following websites contain information about sites in Washington, D.C. many of which are mentioned in this book. The authors believe these will be of great benefit in understanding each place.

Arlington National Cemetery   http://www.arlingtoncemetery.mil/#/
Arlington House: The Robert E Lee Memorial
    https://www.nps.gov/arho/index.htm
Washington DC Travel Site   http://washington.org/
Lincoln Memorial https://www.nps.gov/linc/index.htm
Washington Monument   https://www.nps.gov/wamo/index.htm
Franklin Delano Roosevelt Memorial   https://www.nps.gov/frde/index.htm
Vietnam Veterans Memorial Wall   https://www.nps.gov/vive/index.htm
Martin Luther King, Jr. Memorial   https://www.nps.gov/mlkm/index.htm
World War II Memorial   https://www.nps.gov/wwii/index.htm
The White House   https://www.whitehouse.gov/
The Capitol   https://www.visitthecapitol.gov/
The Smithsonian Institute   http://www.si.edu/
(There is a listing of all the Museums at the site)
The Library of Congress   https://loc.gov/
The Supreme Court   http://www.supremecourt.gov/
Woodrow Wilson House on S Street   http://www.woodrowwilsonhouse.org/
The National Cathedral   http://cathedral.org/
The National Archives   http://www.archives.gov/
The Newseum   http://www.newseum.org/
Ford's Theatre   http://www.fords.org/home/explore-lincoln
Jefferson Memorial   https://www.nps.gov/thje/index.htm
International Spy Museum   http://www.spymuseum.org/
National Gallery of Art   http://www.nga.gov/content/ngaweb.html
Congressional Cemetery   http://www.congressionalcemetery.org/

Made in the USA
Charleston, SC
13 May 2016